OUTDOOR TRUTHS

Hunting and Fishing for Answers

Gary Miller

OUTDOOR TRUTHS

Outdoor Truths, Hunting and Fishing for Answers, is a compilation of articles written over the last few years.

These articles are printed each week in newspapers and regional magazines in 10 states.

ACKNOWLEDGEMENTS

I've found through this process, how much help we all really need in order to accomplish our goals and dreams. Carol Borneman and Linda Lankford have been my two helpers through this process. Carol's red pen has cleaned up my grammatical messes. Linda's organization skills have saved me valuable time. I am truly thankful for both of these ladies.

The pencil drawings are the work of Deborah Golden. Her talent is obvious. I appreciate her contribution.

My wife Teresa, along with our three children, Bethany, Brittany, and Stuart, are what makes me complete. Each has watched me turn my time in the outdoors into a passion to write. Without their love and support, this would not be possible.

The Lord has put within me a love for nature. His creation constantly amazes me. He has allowed me to see Him in new ways from my time outdoors. I cannot be thankful enough.

....The LORD has His way
In the whirlwind and in the storm,
And the clouds are the dust of His feet.
(Nahum 1:3)

***

This book is dedicated to my wife, Teresa.

For 26 years she has endured the life of a hunter and fisherman. This has been the easy part. The hard part has been living with a dreamer.

I'm saddened many times, when I think of all that I've put her through. I'm so thankful that she has always been the voice of reason.

Her own childhood was full of country living. I have listened intently to her stories about churning butter and "slopping" the hogs. I have laughed as she described a tiny house that held six sisters and a brother. To this day, they love one another.

She was my childhood sweetheart and the only woman that I've ever told that I loved.

INTRODUCTION

An atheist hunter? That's one term I have never heard. I'm sure there is someone out there who would fit this description, but I've never met him. In fact, just the opposite is true. Those who spend their time in the woods or on the water can't help but see God in all creation.

Even though we may have different theological views, all hunters and fisherman can agree on one fact: only God could have created things as wonderful as we see each time we sit in a tree stand, hide in a turkey blind, or cast another bait.

From seeing a squirrel working diligently to get ready for the winter, or watching a family of raccoons move in line like an army platoon, to listening to the familiar low of a mourning dove, there is no doubt about the hand of God upon this earth. Everyone can believe this truth, but a hunter and fisherman see it, and understand it like no other.

That is what these articles are about. I hope to share with you the view of heaven from the perspective of those who spend time in the outdoors. Those of you who hunt and fish will understand. And those of you who don't, perhaps will want to by taking a gun into the woods or a fishing rod to the lake and sitting quietly, away from those things that are man-made, and waiting on God to speak through other things as simple as the sparrows that do not fall to the ground without HIS knowing.

Gary

BUT, I TRIED

My mind floods with the memories of my childhood and the outdoors. Everything I attempted was with excited ignorance. That is, I knew what I wanted to do, but I just didn't know how to do it. The woods behind my house seemed as big as any forest I could imagine. It wasn't until I was older, that I realized it was only about eight or ten acres.

I remember the time I planned on trapping a rabbit. I had watched T.V. and decided the best way to do it was to prop a box up on a stick, attached to a string. That morning, I sneaked into the kitchen and took a handful of lettuce from the "head" my momma had just bought. This would serve as bait. I took my box, my lettuce and my Daisy BB gun and moved with settled determination to the woods. I tied a string to a stick, propped up the box on the stick, put the lettuce under the box and moved as far away as my string would allow.........
about ten feet. I waited….. and waited……and waited…..
and waited. No rabbit. I figured I'd been there about fifteen minutes and that ought to have been plenty of time for any rabbit to seal its doom. I gave up, having gained nothing but a wonderful and priceless memory. I did all I knew to do.

When it comes to living the Christian life, we are all ignorant. There's no doubt that God laughs, at times, at our inability. Yes laughs, even as you may have laughed at my ignorance and inability to catch that rabbit. Friend, God's pleasure doesn't come in our accomplishments but in our passionate effort in doing the best we know how.

"FROM THE CONCRETE JUNGLE"

One of the things I have noticed over the last few years is how many people take the opportunity to hunt and fish for granted. If you're reading this article, you probably live in the "country." You probably don't have to go far to get to a lake or river or a boundary of property that you can hunt. In fact, many of you tell me that it's not an uncommon occurrence to see deer standing in your back yard. If that's the case, you are truly blessed because not everyone has that opportunity.

I recently received an email from a friend who loves to hunt and fish and yet is relegated to living some distance from his passion. He signed the message, "From the concrete jungle." He is not one that takes our outdoor luxuries for granted. His determination is to move away from the paved street of convenience to the dirt road of contentment.

I can remember as a high schooler, telling my parents "I can't wait to move away from this little town. There's just nothing to do." As an adult, that is exactly what keeps me here. It's the opportunity to walk outside and look over the hills and up into the mountains, with nothing else to do. It's knowing there are more deer crossing signs than there are red lights and that, at any time, the smell of fresh cow manure may come from one side of the street while the smell of a Hardee's hamburger may come from the other. For an outdoorsman, it is a wonderful dichotomy. I have said many times that I was built for the woods. I still believe that. And what a shame it would be, to be somewhere I don't belong.

God has built a place for all of us. We all have a special calling we are meant to perform. Many times it's found as we look deep within our souls to the longings that surface.

To remain where we're at brings discontentment and dissatisfaction and causes us to respond, "From the concrete jungle."

THE SHADOW OF DEATH

This time of year, the sun is a real friend. It's our only source of heat on a cold day, if you are on the water or in the woods. There have been many times I have closed my eyes, lifted my head, and pointed my face toward that fiery ball just to gather in all of its warmth. The valleys are always the last to receive its benefit because of the shadows of the mountains and trees. The shadows, however, are no threat to the sun. With enough time, they too will be conquered. Even though shadows may hinder, they can never hurt. And even though they may look large, as the sun rises, they become smaller and smaller. No one can ever say they have been injured by a shadow.

I have been in the woods several times when trees have fallen. Sometimes they have come so close the shadow literally crossed my body, but the shadow left me unharmed. Let me ask you: "Had you rather be hit by that big white oak, or its shadow?" That's easy. We had rather be hit by the shadow because the shadow can't hurt us.

There is a very familiar chapter in the Bible. It's Psalm 23. You, perhaps, have heard it read in a funeral or wedding or some other occasion. It begins like this. "The lord is my shepherd, I shall not want. He makes me lie die down in green pastures." And then on down in the chapter it says this. "Yea, though I walk through the valley of the *shadow* of death, I will fear no evil, for You are with me." Did you notice what it said? Not the "valley of death," but the "valley of the *shadow* of death."

You see, God made a way for those who would receive His son, to not have to go through death as we know it, but only its shadow. Are you grieving over someone right now? Don't grieve as those who have no hope, because just as the shadows of a falling tree cannot hurt you, neither can the shadows of death for those who are allowing the Lord to walk through the valley with them.

FRIENDS AND FISHERMEN

S ome of my most vivid memories come from the days of being on the lake. And just because they are vivid, doesn't mean all of them are good. I can remember catching stripe bass as fast as I could cast but I can also remember being scared to death because I had not left early enough to beat the lightening storm. It seems that we always think there's enough time for one more throw.

As I got older, I began to value my life more. Now, if there's a storm within a hundred miles, I leave. There's just something about holding a graphite rod in my hand, in the middle of a lake, that doesn't sit well with me.

Most of my memories, however, are good. They include days on a bass boat, a pontoon, and even wading. What all of them have in common is that the greatest moments were shared with someone who was there, whether a friend, one of my children or even a stranger.

It was with these friends that I learned to eat potted meat, Vienna sausage and pork n' beans. This is stuff we never eat any other time.

I have learned, if you're fishing with a friend, it's ok to hold a bologna sandwich with the same hand that just "lipped" that big bass. (In case you didn't know, there are no germs on the lake.)

Yes, friends are what I like about fishing. I don't have to be anything, but what I am.

Jesus was known as a friend of sinners. He even called fishermen to follow him. I'm glad, because I am both. In fact, I am all three. I'm a fisherman, a sinner AND a follower of Jesus.

THE WALLEYE RUN

Several years ago, I can remember going down to the river during late winter to try my hand during the walleye run. Only until the other day, I had forgotten how much fun it really was.

I had the opportunity to go back with my former high school basketball coach. He is a nut about fishing, and his specialty is walleye. We spent all day jigging for this wonderful table delicacy. We brought home 7 keepers. I was sure glad he let me take them all home, and no one at my house complained about supper that night.

Coach is on the list of the retired whose work now is fishing on every day that ends in "Y." While some are still in the "getting and gaining" mode, these men are pursuing the simple contentment that comes from being on one end of a rod or gun. Another retiree told me just last week, that "every day is Saturday." He loves life. He also admonished me to make sure I keep my son hunting and fishing so he will stay out of trouble. He told me his son, who is now raising his own family, lives on the lake and fishes everyday. He is so proud of that.

You see, to these men, their boat was more than a tool to catch fish, but it was a place where the awkwardness of a conversation between a father and his child became easy. Over the years, the lake or the river had become a place where counseling, advice, and even prayers were offered. It was a place where major decisions were contemplated and settled. It was there that interruptions were welcomed if they were of the fish variety. And it was there that smiles were real and honest.

It seems that "us men" need help in communicating at times. We struggle with the right words and tone of voice, and even timing. The fishing trip knocks the edge off of all of that and allows us to spoon feed words of wisdom to those who must grow up, and old, and to those who need to "stay out of trouble."

RESPONDING TO A CALL

I can remember an old Krystal's commercial that had a
police officer pulling over a vehicle for some violation.
When the officer came to the driver's window, it seemed that
the driver was in a trance. His excuse for the violation and
the trance was the thought of a bag of Krystal burgers. And
his words were…….. "I'm just responding to a call."

Every so often I notice myself and even others acting in a
way that is abnormal. It usually happens when we want to go
hunting or fishing but we can't. There's some other obliga-
tion or obstacle that's standing in the way. To make matters
worse, a friend will call and tell you that the boat is hooked
up and he's ready to go. This inevitably causes the wheels to
start turning in our mind to see if there is any way possible
that we can finagle our present circumstances into a way to
go fishing. This is, most of the time, a "no-win" situation. If
we stay home, we're cranky, irritable and have no attention
span. If we go fishing, we never catch a fish and we know
somebody at home is not going to be happy that we went.
The scenario is familiar to all of us.

So what is it that causes us to act, or react, in such a way?
We're just responding to a call. There's something within
each of us that is triggered when our particular passion is
mentioned. It's the hot button that overrides all common
sense and direction. It takes normally sane human beings
and brings us back to the days of being the hunter or gath-
erer. The only way we can explain it is …… we are just
responding to a call.

God has put another passion within each of us. It is a desire to know the ONE who can create this outdoor world that we love so much. It starts as a young child, when we ask "Mommy, who made the stars?" or "Daddy, who made the mountains?" Some spend a lifetime trying to answer that question without ever satisfying the urge within them. But the ones who are "responding to the call" are the ones who have reconciled that the same God who created the heavens and the earth and all that is within them, can also live within me.

BIRD DOGS

Have you ever seen a dog "work?" I mean have you ever seen a dog in the woods, "point" a grouse or a pheasant? It is truly an amazing sight. They pick up the smell, follow it to the bird, stand still with tail extended and one front foot in the air until the bird flies or until you get there to kick it up.

Dogs and hunting go hand in hand for many outdoorsmen. To them, a good dog is more important than a good gun. They spend time training and coaching. Some even pay lots of money to send their dog away to someone who specializes in getting it ready to hunt. I love seeing a good dog work.

The experiences with my own hunting dogs are not quite the same. Mine is more of a religious experience. That is, I about lose my religion every time I try to make a dog learn to hunt. Since I never had any "learnin" when it comes to training dogs, I use to try whatever seemed good to me at the time. I have tied long ropes to hold them; carried feathers from dead grouse to let them know what we're looking for and have even carried with me a handful of treats to reward them when they did well. It seems, however, the only thing that worked and the only thing that gave *me* satisfaction was to unload a 12 gauge 7 shot in their behind. (I feel better just talking about it) Now before you call PETA or the Humane Society, I just want you to know that I have *never* shot a *good* dog! (Okay, I really never even shot a *bad* one.)

There is one thing however, that I never doubted about any dog that I have ever owned, and that is, they all wanted

25

to please me. And knowing that, made me love every one of them even when they failed.

Friend, God is not interested in the quality of your performance, but in your heart's desire to please Him.

TURKEYS OR EAGLES

I was reminded last week, how close we are to turkey season. (As if I didn't already know) There, in the field, were a flock of birds with one lone gobbler blown up as big as it could get. It was just standing there, nose in the air, as if to say, "Look at me everybody."

Even though I love turkey hunting, there's something about that big tom that always reminds me of the little people in life. You know.............. the "little" people. The ones who are "puffed" up, who strut around, and who try to make themselves look like something they're not. They are actually little, but they make themselves up to be big. That's exactly what that old tom was doing in that field. And it just might be what gets him his head blown off in a few weeks! Now, don't get me wrong. I know that, unless I treat these "proud" people well, I am no better than they, but it still bothers me when I see this hypocrisy.

I have heard in times past, some who thought America's symbol should have been the turkey. After all, it was plentiful during the days of our beginning, and it is known for its adaptability. And it's been a part of our Thanksgiving heritage for years. But no; I still prefer the good old eagle. It's the bird that chooses to fly above all of the strutting and posturing. It's the bird that doesn't try to be something that it's not and it's the bird whose nose stays in the middle of his face. Am I saying that America is all of these things? Absolutely not. But I am saying that I had rather strive to be like that eagle than the turkey.

Here's what the scriptures say about the antics of the turkey. "Love suffers long *and* is kind; love does not envy; love does not parade itself, is not puffed up." And here is what the scriptures say about the eagle.

"But those who wait on the Lord
Shall renew *their* strength;
They shall mount up with wings like eagles,
They shall run and not be weary,
They shall walk and not faint." Yep, I believe I need to spend more of my time hunting turkeys and trying to be more like tagles.

READING OR JUST RENEWING

I have to admit that one of my weaknesses is hunting and fishing magazines. They are all over the house and never too far out of reach. There are Field and Stream, Outdoor Life, American Hunter, North American Hunter, Tennessee Valley Outdoors, Tennessee Wildlife, River Country, and The Christian Bowhunter. And that's not including the ones that "happen" to be at the check-out counter, that I have to have, when I'm leaving the grocery store. Now, please don't give my name to anybody else if you're reading this. I have a hard time saying no, especially if it's "$2.00 off the newsstand price." Yes, I confess, these are my weaknesses. Some like Twinkies, others like donuts, but I love outdoor magazines.

The only problem is I never read them on a consistent basis. I look forward to them each month, I ask my wife if she has forgotten to get them out of the back seat of her car, and during certain parts of the year I am more interested. But when it's all said and done, I only fiddle through them, most of the time. But when it's time to renew....... absolutely! And if someone were to ask me to give up these morsels of pleasure, I would cry heresy! It's sort of like when we men take a nap on the couch with a ballgame on; we might be snoring loud enough to wake the neighbors, but if someone tries to change the channel, we wake up immediately. Now you understand.

When I think about this scenario, I realize that this is the way most of us do our Bibles. They are in our living room, the dining room and even on the night stand. They are always within reach. If someone were to try to take these from our possession, we would take up arms. But when we stand back and think about it, we rarely ever read it. I know in those outdoor magazines are words of advice from some of the leading experts in their fields, and if I would only read them, I would become a better hunter or fisherman. In the Bible are words even greater than those; words that not only make life better but actually give new life to those who need and read it.

PRIDE COMES BEFORE THE FALL

When I think about turkey season, so many thoughts run through my mind. I think of making sure I'm in shape enough to climb the mountains of my home area. I think of hearing that first gobble coming from the dark skies on a chilly April morning. And I think of the joy of "talking turkey" with the resident toms. It's fun, it's challenging, and it's very rewarding, especially when I can "bring home the bacon." (Umm, I mean the turkey.)

Details are important when hunting turkey. Full camouflage is a must. When that gobbler comes in, there can be no movement. And calling must not be too aggressive and not too light. But, if everything goes right, pride will be his downfall. Yes, pride.

You see, a tom likes to strut. He will fan his tail, stick out his chest, and pace back and forth in order to impress the lady hens. His demise comes when he mistakes the call of a hen for the call of a hunter. When he begins strutting in front of a hunter, he is blinded by his preoccupation with himself. He cannot see around his own plumage. It's an amazing array of self-involvement. This move gives me just enough time to hold him tightly within the sights of my shotgun, and pull the trigger. Pride came before the fall.

What a reminder he is to my own daily life. What a picture of the results of trying to "strut" for those who are calling my name. The Bible says, "For I say to everyone who is among you, not to think of himself more highly than he ought to think." This doesn't mean that we degrade ourselves, only that we make sure pride does not blind us to the things that will cause us to fall.

HERE'S YOUR SIGN!

It seems like every area of life deals with signs. There used to be a popular song that went like this. "Signs, signs, everywhere signs; blocking up the scenery, breaking up my mind. Do this, don't do that, can't you read the signs."

And then there's the ever popular phrase ...... "Here's your sign!"

Let me try one.

I was going to speak at the funeral of a dear older lady and someone stopped me as I was leaving. They asked... "Where ya goin?" And I said, "To speak at the funeral of sister "so and so". To which they replied, with surprise ...... "Did she die?" To which I replied, "No, but I'm going to be out of town when she does, so I figured I would just do it now!" "Here's your sign!"

We hunters are also looking for signs. They tell us where the turkeys are hanging out during certain parts of the day and where they are spending their nights. Signs are important.

They are important to God too. In fact, this time of year we celebrate Easter, the resurrection of Jesus. But in our outdoor world, God also gives us signs that tell us that one day we all will be raised from the dead, to life. Every time the sun goes down, it signifies a death. But the rising of the sun signifies a resurrection. Recently, the trees and plants have been without bloom, and seemingly without life. This signifies death. But now they all are sprouting, signifying a resurrection. Each night when my eyes close, I am signifying a death, but when I rise in the morning, I am signifying a resurrection. So you see, God does give us signs. They are here for us to see and to know and to understand what God, the Creator and Savior of the universe, is up to in our lives and in the world.

THE CALLOUSES OF BEING FAITHFUL

If you look at most of my hunting and fishing trips from the standpoint of harvesting game, you would conclude that I was unsuccessful. Most of the time, I leave home with great expectations, only to return with the reality of an unfilled tag or an empty live well.

I remember a commercial where a man's wife watched her husband leave each Saturday morning with his fishing rod and Labrador, only to come back home that afternoon, with just his fishing rod and his faithful companion. She wondered why he continued to go. I can also remember, the days when my children were young, that I would return home from a hunting trip and would be faced by three children with the same question: "Did you get anything?" They got so used to the same answer, they began not to ask. (I'm sure glad that our sustenance was not based on me bringing home the meat) But, what I found out over the years was that I did not become a better hunter or fisherman on days that the harvest was easy, but I became better, most of the time, on the days that I came home empty-handed.

Let's face it; it doesn't take much know-how to go out and catch fish when they are biting everything that comes in front of them. Nor is much knowledge gained when that deer meanders by your treestand 10 minutes after daylight. Knowledge to become a better outdoorsman is gained through the tough times. It happens when we shoot high on that deer or don't set the hook on that bass. It's those times that we come home "better" than when we left, whether we have something to show for it or not. And even though we want to fill a tag, it's *better* to come home *better*.

This is also the way God works. God is not interested in what we do, or what we "harvest" at the expense of what we are becoming. He is interested in us being *better*. Better husbands or wives, better fathers or mothers, and better Christians. This doesn't happen during the easy days but during the days when there is nothing in our hands to show for our effort except the calluses of being faithful.

LUCKY OR BLESSED?

I was sitting in McDonalds, with my son, after a morning of turkey hunting. I was "wolfing" down the deluxe breakfast. We had walked a few miles earlier and were in need of some nutrition. I didn't ask about "carbs" or "points" when I saw the picture of those pancakes, sausage and eggs, only how soon I could get it.

My turkey hunting place is not like you see on T.V. It's steep, mountainous and very trying on a man of 29 plus...... Alright, plus a lot! We had climbed and descended several times, trying to locate a willing gobbler. The responses were distant and willing to stay that way. At the end of the morning, we had managed only to call in a hen.

Back to McDonalds..........

There we were when a friendly older stranger asked, "Did you have any luck?" And in a second of time, I analyzed that seemingly simple question. I knew what he wanted to know, but my thoughts went in so many other directions. I finally said, "Well, we didn't kill a turkey." In reality, it was so much more than that to me, on that day. I thought about the beautiful, cool, crisp, sunny day that I had enjoyed. I recalled the tree covered hills that we had climbed and the fact that I was doing what I loved to do and I was doing it with my son. Did I have any luck? Some would say I was the luckiest man on earth. I say, I was blessed.

I'm not sure about luck. Luck seems to omit God. I had rather see Him in control of the events of my life, no matter how small. Blessings give me someone to thank. And I had much rather thank God, than to thank my lucky stars.

THAT CANTANKOROUS TOM

There's nothing like the sound of a gobble at daylight. If you're close enough, it seems that it reverberates throughout the hollows and ridges. It will truly make you wide awake like nothing else. The method most of us use to cause a tom to gobble is by using some kind of shock call. For you non-turkey hunters, a shock call is simply a loud noise that is made that causes a gobbler to react to the sound by gobbling. There are also other calls that are used like an owl hoot. I'm not totally sure, but I think that the turkey despises the old hoot owl so much that when they hear one, they just fuss back at it by gobbling. But whether you shock one or owl hoot or crow call, the results are the same; a turkey is located.

It seems to me that the old gobbler is a cantankerous bird. When something unexpected happens, he fusses. When some other creature wants to sing out, he fusses. When something is different or interrupts his normal routine, he fusses. But what he doesn't realize is that by his responses and reactions, he lets everyone know where he is. And in turkey hunting, that's good for the hunter and not good for him.

He sort of reminds me of some people I know. They are fine when everything goes their way and when everything is as it should be, and when there are no unexpected interruptions or unplanned circumstances. But when something happens that is out of the ordinary, they fuss and complain. It may be the clerk at the grocery store who smashes his bread or the waitress at the restaurant who gets his order wrong, but, again, the results are the same. What he doesn't realize is that by his actions, he is letting everyone know where he is. He is telling the world around him that what you see might not be what you get. He is telling everyone what is really inside. I think that he forgets about his own imperfections and his own mental lapses. He seems to demand more from others than he does from himself. I hope that you're not that way, because the true test of Christian character is not how we act during the expected but how we react when we are shocked by the unexpected.

HE GAVE IN TO TEMPTATION

While deer hunting for the most part is lying in wait for an unsuspecting deer, turkey hunting is lying in wait for a turkey that is well aware that there is a presence up ahead. The problem arises for him when his expectations are not realized. It's the sound of the lonesome hen that has lured him away from the safety and surety of his flock. A good hunter is able to draw the gobbler away by placing in his mind the pleasure that lies over the next hill.

Even though it doesn't always work, the scenario is a very familiar one. It is the lure of greener pastures. It comes from the sounds that tell him what he wants to hear. It's the soft, subtle and sexy voice of the opposite sex. It says come on over here. It's better here. There are no problems here. You will be appreciated and understood here. And thousands each year respond to that call. The wise old toms live and love another year with those that he has been with time and time again.

Under each picture of our turkey successes, ought to be written, "He gave in to temptation." After all, that is exactly what he did. Isn't it? We can analyze it, dissect it, and put it into easy hunting words, but the fact is still the same....... He was drawn away by temptation, and there he got more than he bargained for.

Hunter friend, let these experiences be a lesson to all of us. Perhaps, right now, you are hearing the sounds of the lonesome hen or lonesome gobbler. They are coming from a place that you cannot see. They say all the right things about how better it is over here compared to where you are right now. To give in will be to get more than you bargained for. Instead, go home to the place that is safe and sure. Hug the one that God gave you. Live and love another day.

THOSE MARVOULOUS MORELS

O nce again, this time of year, the Hickory Chicken hunters are in prime shape. I had my first mess of these delicious morels just the other day. I still can't get over how much I love these things, and yet they are so hard to find. One hunter told me "there seems to be no rhyme or reason for finding them." I agree. Even though there are certain areas that I look for initially, I have found these mushrooms on the mountain top and in the hollows, with no rhyme or reason. It reminds me of a story in the Bible. One about a man named Boaz and a woman named Ruth.

Boaz was very rich and Ruth was very poor. In fact she was so poor that she would glean the crop fields of Boaz just to find enough leftovers to survive on. If one of Boaz's workers dropped grain they were not allowed to pick it up. That was the Jewish law. This helped to take care of the poor. Boaz however began to fall in love with Ruth, so he would have his workers drop some grain on purpose or "for no rhyme or reason." This assured that Ruth and her mother would have enough. He told his field workers to leave some "handfuls on purpose." As in any good love story, they married and lived happily ever after. It is a truly wonderful story to read.

When I think about these mushrooms that we find in the woods, I think that God just has some of his angels leave some "handfuls on purpose" this time of year. They seem to be special blessings that are scattered throughout with no rhyme or reason. They are left for those who will glean the fields. Sometimes there are but a few and sometimes it seems that God has had his special workers leave a whole basket. Either way, I'm glad that even though some have learned to farm these treats, the good ones are still grown by a God who is rich in mercy and goodness and they are given, freely, to a people who are dependant upon that same goodness and mercy.

WHO NEEDED WHO?

One Saturday, I had the privilege of taking part in the National Wild Turkey Federation's Wheelin' Sportsmen's hunt. The Wheelin' Sportsmen is an arm of the NWTF that provides an opportunity for the disabled to get out and enjoy hunting and fishing and other events. This particular event was sponsored by three regional chapters. Over 20 disabled hunters came to participate in a turkey hunt. Along with those hunters, were people like me, who were teamed up with them in order to help while in the turkey blind.

My hunting partners were Rick and his disabled older brother, Terry. Terry is 46 years old. He had been in a car wreck only three years ago. And, as a result of that accident, was left paralyzed from his waist, down. He had been a deer hunter, and had even taken a deer after his accident. But, this was his first time in the turkey woods. I really don't know who was more excited about our hunt; me, Rick, or Terry.

Rick cared for his brother with a special compassion. His love for him was evident. He wanted nothing more than his big brother to harvest a gobbler. I wish the turkeys would have been more cooperative. As I sat with them that morning, I realized that I would be the one who would receive the biggest blessing from this trip.

It was Terry who praised God for his life. He was thankful that his life had been spared and was quick to add that God had a plan. No bitterness, no anger, no unanswered questions; only a deep and sincere gratitude............

One that confronted me, and my unwarranted whining. One that caused me to hunker down, expecting at any time, for God to slap me across the face. And one that put things back in the right perspective.

I sat in that blind for hours. My back ached. My legs cried to be stretched. What a wonderful blessing. After the hunt was over, Rick and I stood and walked, and stretched. Terry couldn't. He was still confined to a wheel chair. The temptation was to feel sorry for him. The truth was, I was the one who this hunt was for. I was the one who needed help. I was the one who needed someone who was capable of doing for me, what I was unable to do for myself.

A GUN AND A GIFT

Recently, my youngest turned sixteen. Not many days after that, he was driving on his own. I'm sure that he will have a lasting memory of this time. The memory of my turning sixteen is much different. It's not of girls, cars, or school, but of guns. At sixteen years of age, I bought my first shotgun. It is, no doubt, the most vivid memory I have of that age. I will never forget going into the sporting goods department at Roses and purchasing a single shot, sixteen gauge, Stevens shotgun. They didn't ask for I.D. They didn't do a background check. They simply took my fifty dollars and I took home my gun.

That may not seem like a big deal to some, but for me it was monumental. Because my father never hunted, guns were not a part of our home. When I bought that gun, I never thought of revenge for all of the times I had been the blunt of every "skinny" joke. I never thought of getting back at a teacher or someone that I didn't like, or any other of the nonsense that adults assume normal kids will do when they get a gun. I just thought about hunting. But, I will never forget the feeling that I had when I walked out of that store and put that gun in my car. I felt like a man! I felt that I had arrived. I felt like I had found and restored a part of me that had been missing for so long. I remember that feeling like it was yesterday.

That's what happens when we come to Christ. We become a new man. We arrive at the place we were meant to be. And, that missing part of our life is found and restored. It is unexplainable until you step in God's storehouse yourself and receive the gift that is waiting for everyone.

A SIMPLE POCKET KNIFE

O ne of the tools of those who love the outdoors is a knife. There has always been something special about getting a new knife. I see that same satisfaction in my son. He owns several and is never unhappy when he receives another. It's almost a rite of passage when a young man gets his first. Some weaker types cringe at the thought of their son having a knife. I cringe at the thought of them cringing over such a common and natural thing.

I have several warm memories of my youth experiences with knives. One of them involved Tom. Tom was a man in his upper seventies and I was only a teenager. Tom was wise and crafty. I was dumb and naive. Tom had more knives than I could ever imagine. Some of them use to be mine, until he traded me out of them. At that time, I thought that I had made the smarter trade. Today, I know different. Tom couldn't read or write but had more common sense and wisdom most of the people that I knew. He was also a very spiritual man. His ministry involved making sure that each home had been dedicated to the Lord. If it hadn't, he would gather a small congregation and meet at the willing participant's house on a Saturday night. There, someone would give a biblical lesson or preach a sermon, a song would be sung and Tom would offer a prayer of dedication.

Some in my home area are still living in a house that has been dedicated to the Lord by Tom. There were several times that I was the one called on to speak. I learned so much from him. I laugh now when I think about how he would "horse trade" with me. But he was doing so much more than "horse trading." He was "growing up" a young man. He was teaching me the cunning ways of the world and the caring ways of the Lord. And he was not doing it with something that might have caused me to run away. But he was doing it with something that caused me to want to be around him and something that we both loved; a knife.

READY FOR THE CALL

I have always been an early bird. It seems that if I get up after daybreak, I've missed something. I've always been intrigued by the way each day starts. Every Sunday morning, for over ten years, I have taken the drive down the Powell Valley. I try to do this just after first light. It's then, that I get to see the outdoors at its best. The blend of the orange sun peeking over the green mountains, with the backdrop of blue skies and white clouds, is a perfectly painted picture. And there is always something special about the smell and taste of the cool air after it has been filtered by the night.

For those many years, I have always been greeted by the animals that are making the transition from night to day. The deer are going to the safe and secluded confines of home, while the Tom turkey is stretching and strutting in full open sight. I cross paths with the coyote, fox, and raccoon. And because of the reintroduction of the elk to our area, perhaps maybe this September, the valley will reverberate with the sounds of the bull's bugle. I can't imagine what that will sound like, the first time I hear it. But, I'm ready. I'm expecting it. I will know what it is.

One day that same valley, and every valley, will ring with another sound. It will be a bugle, but not one made by an animal or man. It will come from the trumpet of Gabriel. It will announce the coming of Christ. And even though I have never heard it before, I've been expecting it. I'm ready. I will know what it is.

Friend, the reintroduction of Christ is coming to your area too. You may be caught unaware, but you don't have to be caught unprepared.

A TURTLE AND
A FRUIT TREE

I was driving home the other day and happened to run up on a man standing on the edge of the road, watching a large snapping turtle as it was attempting to cross in his direction. Since it was on a back road, I stopped. I knew what he was doing. He was wanting to catch, kill, clean, cook, and fry that odd delicacy. How did I know? I have done the same thing. That sight brought back another memory of days past.

I can remember as a teenager ganging up on one of these critters with the other "boys in the hood." After catching a large turtle, we took it to the home of a couple that had endeared themselves to our little group. There, I watched as Johnny cleaned it and Liz fried it, and each one of us youngsters tasted our first turtle. I can remember that I really liked it. What did it taste like? Chicken, of course! Well, not really. I think it tasted like turtle, but I had never eaten turtle to know how turtle was supposed to taste. I had, however, eaten a lot of chicken.

It was at that time that I was told that a turtle was made up of seven different kinds of meat. It was not until recently that I learned that only two kinds actually reside inside that shell; white meat and dark meat. (You guessed it......just like chicken)

Even though the story of seven different kinds of meat is a myth, there is a tree that the Bible talks about that has twelve different kinds of fruit. It's not found in any particular country or climate. It's not even found on this earth........... yet. One day, however, there will be a new earth and a new city. Within that city will be a river. And on each side of that river will be a tree of life that bears twelve different kinds of fruit EVERY MONTH! Who wouldn't want to live there? You can. It's called heaven. And it was created for all who will come by the way of the cross.

DISSAPOINTMENTS

I was not raised in a hunting or fishing family. It seems what I learned was either from the "gang" or simply from the desire I had to hunt and fish. When I was young, the only fishing I ever did was around town at the canals. During that time, the tackle of choice was a Zebco 202 and a 25 cent can of whole kernel corn. I was a carp fisherman. But I was good! I mean if there would have been a carpmasters' classic, I would have been on the tour. I have spent many mornings with the canal in front of me and the drive up window at the old National Bank behind me. It didn't seem to bother me that people were going and coming as I was fishing for the only fish I had ever caught.......a carp.

At the age of 15 I took my first trip to the lake with a Royal Ambassador church group. I couldn't wait to get there. I planned for that day by buying a Rapala crank bait. Finally, after all the years of catching carp, I was going to catch a bass from the lake. I was the first one off the bus. I ran down to the lake and began casting. It only took a few casts before I had a fish on the other end. The rest of the group gathered around to watch me land that large-mouth bass. But there was only one problem. At the other end of that line, there was not the bass that I had dreamed of catching. It was.... you guessed it, a carp.

What a disappointment!

Life is full of disappointments. They come to young and old. They are big and small. But remember, the disappointments of the past are never meant to keep us from becoming what we are supposed to become now and in the future. God is greater than all of our disappointments.

THE FRY IT DIET

This time of year I always try catching some pan fish. I really enjoy this slow, unhurried outdoor activity. It's especially good after managing the deadlines of deer and turkey seasons, and an occasional bass tournament. There are no seasons for bluegill and crappie. If today is unsuccessful, maybe I'll go tomorrow; or maybe not. And there is nothing like fried fish from these varieties. Yes, fried.

I remember the days when there was no such a thing as calories, carbohydrates and cholesterol. At least I didn't know there was. Now, it seems that anything that is fried is bad for me. I really wish I could fry the guy who found that out. He's probably a vegetarian too! Which I heard is an old Indian word for "bad hunter." But, it looks like he's right. And I really hate that.

Have you ever noticed that you can put anything in a pan of hot grease and it will come out tasting good? We use to save grease just for frying things. That's what that ceramic jar on the stove was for. And how many of you can remember "killing" some fresh lettuce and onions in bacon grease and following that up with a piece of *fried* cornbread with real butter on it? Try to find that on somebody's menu today. No, today if we eat lettuce and onions it will be on a salad with a tablespoon of some kind of fat free dressing. And that cornbread turned into a club cracker. No wonder the crime level has escalated in America! I'd be mad too if somebody swapped my cornbread for a cracker!

And I just read the other day that obesity in America has reached epidemic levels. Why? I don't know. But I know that it wasn't that way when I had my jar of grease on the stove!

Have you ever noticed when grease is put in food it holds that particular food together? It doesn't matter if it's cake or hamburger; grease holds it together. Now I think there's a great parallel here that we need to see. Have you noticed how our world is falling apart? Yep, that's right. It happened when we took the grease out.

Oh, the ramblings of those who hate to diet.

UNASHAMED

There's no doubt that what we do make an impression on our young people and those who look up to us. Just as I remember buying my first new gun, I also remember my first new knife. Not only was I enamored by the knife itself, but I was also very interested in the paperwork that came with it. While most would only throw away the unnecessary stuff, I made it a point to find out about my new Buck knife. It talked about how to take care of it and how to sharpen it. But what caught my attention was the message from Al Buck. It read like this.

Now that you are family, you might like to know a little more about our organization. The fantastic growth of Buck Knives was no accident. From the beginning, management determined to make God the Senior Partner. In a crisis, the problem was turned over to Him, and He hasn't failed to help us with the answer. Each product must reflect the integrity of management, including our Senior Partner. If sometimes we fail on our end, because we are human, we find it imperative to do our utmost to make it right. Of course, to us, besides being Senior Partner, He is our Heavenly Father also; and it's a great blessing to us to have this security in these troubled times. If any of you are troubled or perplexed and looking for answers, may we invite you to look to Him, for God loves you.

"For God so loved the world that he gave His only begotten son; that whoever believeth in Him should not perish, but have everlasting life." John: 3:16

Wow! What an impression that made on a teenager. I thought that "big" companies and "successful" people surely had no need for God. I was wrong, and I never forgot that simple message purposefully placed in that little box. Twenty five years later, every time I go to buy a knife, I'm reminded of that day that someone cared enough to be unashamed of their faith and who also understood that all that we have and all that we do is to be used to reflect the goodness and the grace of a Heavenly Father.

SELECTIVE SPINAL DISFUNCTION

Over the past few years, I have noticed a remarkable phenomenon that was again, brought to my attention just the other day. I have noticed that I can walk for hours and miles across mountains and through the woods, and even though I may get tired, my back and legs never ache. But put me in a mall or in a grocery store with my wife, and in about 15 minutes, I am begging her to call 911. My back aches, my legs throb and pretty soon I am looking for one of those mall tree stands, called a bench. I'm sure there are more people out there just like me. Perhaps we need to start a support group or something. My wife says my back hurts when I want it to. I prefer to say I have selective spinal dysfunction. I have noticed, however, a cessation of pain when I get around the sporting goods department in Wal-Mart.

There is no doubt that more men would shop if the floors were made of dirt and at least one item of camouflage was in every aisle. Or perhaps if they strategically placed a deer decoy at certain places and we were asked to judge the yardage. If there were 25 aisles, there would be 25 deer. And the one closest to the exact yardage at the end of the "hunt" would get a free subscription to Field and Stream. Now *that's* how to get me to go shopping with my wife!

It also seems that, many times, we outdoorsmen have a selective sickness on Sundays. While we will go hunting or fishing with pneumonia, we'll skip church at the first sign of a hangnail. Our excuses fool no one, including God. If we all were as determined to be in church as we are to be in the woods or on the lake, we would be known as one of God's most faithful people.

BE STILL

It seems that no matter which outdoor sport you choose, it involves stillness. Whether you are sitting in a tree stand, luring in a gobbler, or wetting a line, the antsy outdoorsman is the one who goes home hungry. On the other hand, the successful one is, more than likely, the one who has learned to be still. Have you ever noticed how sensitive to our surroundings we are when we are still? Not inactive, but patiently and expectantly still. The lightest tug of that largemouth is transferred throughout the whole body. The slightest movement in the woods seems like a rude interruption. And the faintest sound is as loud as an alarm clock; all because we have chosen to be still.

Stillness is not natural. We come from the womb kicking and screaming. Our childhood is made up of one activity after another. I can still remember my first trip to the barber and how hard it was to be still. We spend our school days squirming around like a puppy hoping that our teacher doesn't see our activity and tell us to be "still." No, stillness is not natural, but it is necessary. It is necessary in every area of our lives, including our spiritual life. Moses told the children of Israel as they came to the Red Sea, "Stand still and see the salvation of the Lord." He also told them, "Stand still that I may hear what the Lord will command concerning you." And, as God spoke to Elijah, the Bible says,

Then He said, "Go out, and stand on the mountain before the LORD." And behold, the LORD passed by, and a great and strong wind tore into the mountains and broke the rocks in pieces before the LORD, *but* the LORD *was* not in the wind;

and after the wind an earthquake, *but* the LORD *was* not in the earthquake; and after the earthquake a fire, *but* the LORD *was* not in the fire; and after the fire a still small voice.

It was in that "still small voice" that the Lord was heard. And it is the same way today. That's what I like about hunting and fishing. They teach me what is unnatural........ to be still. And if I can be still at these activities, I can also be still long enough to hear the "still small voice" of God giving me direction and encouragement and wisdom for what lies ahead.

THE SNAKE AND THE BOTTLE

One of my childhood memories was going blackberry picking. I can remember gathering up buckets and jugs, heading to a hidden thicket and picking those delicious morsels until my hands and my mouth had both turned purple. Mom would clean and freeze them, and we would eat cobbler for the year.

One day, my dad gathered my brother and me for this chore. We drove to meet others at the foot of the mountain. Our destination was the strip road at the top of the mountain. As we crossed the railroad tracks and entered the woods, there, lying on the ground was a man with a shotgun propped up across his chest and an empty whiskey bottle beside him. He had no doubt passed out. As a youngster, I was a little scared. I was not used to seeing such a sight. We moved on quietly up the mountain. But as you see, I never forgot that picture. When we finally arrived at the top, I was immediately taken back by bush after bush full of blackberries. My dad, however, was taken back by the sight of a rattlesnake that was sunning just a few steps away. This was another sight I had never seen.

As a child, I never correlated my two new experiences. As an adult, I did.

The Proverbs say:

"Who has woe?

Who has sorrow?

Who has contentions?

Who has complaints?

Who has wounds without cause?
Who has redness of eyes?
Those who linger long at the wine."

And then it says:
"At the last it bites like a serpent,
And stings like a viper."

There's no doubt that sometime earlier, that snake had made its way from the top of that mountain to the drunk below. He had slithered just close enough to deposit his venom into that bottle. He cleverly disguised it with a nice label. But the proof of the real substance was lying there, unable to move, or stand or comprehend that the real danger was not the snake, but the bottle.

LEARN OR GET LEFT

Growing up in a non hunting/fishing home may have kept me from taking for granted this great privilege.

Today I'm more enthused about the outdoors than any other time in my life. There is still so much to learn about it all. My recent fishing trips have reminded me of this.

There are very few fishermen who go after more than one or two species. Most bass fishermen are just that; bass fisherman. Whether it's February or August, they are still pursuing that bass. Walleye fishermen are set on finding walleye. And the list goes on. But in order to expand our horizon, we must be willing to forget the past, ignore our inability, and set out to learn. To learn, however, is dangerous. It exposes our weaknesses and makes us vulnerable. It highlights the fact that we are not the "super outdoorsman" that others may think we are.

Sometimes we are unwilling to learn because we too, were not raised in that particular environment, and thus we are unwilling to try. To fail to learn means that we're going to fall behind.

Here's an example.

Several years ago, I took a fishing trip to Alabama. We actually went to crappie fish, but it was slow so that we reverted to catching bass. At that time I had never heard of a Carolina rig. Very few had. But I was introduced to the "hows" while I was there. I caught fish but the method was very awkward for someone who was raised "Texas" style. I decided to leave that technique in Alabama. Little did I know that soon after that, the Carolina boom would begin.

At home, tournaments began to be won with a Carolina rig. I stubbornly held to my Texas style worm. My convictions sounded good, but they were convictions with no substance. I simply refused to forget the past and learn.

We all can bring up past pain. We can wallow in the pit of our bad childhood or corrupt environment or a host of other things. And while these are real, they don't have to control your life now. You can choose to adapt and overcome or stubbornly hold on to the ways of the past. And it's all in being willing to learn and expose your weaknesses so that others can show you a new and better way.

WAIT FOR THE TUG

There's nothing like barreling down the lake in the summer at 5:00 in the morning. The cool mist will wake up anybody. But it's not really the air that is alarming, it's the possibility of a big bass that is ready for breakfast; buzz bait style. To see the calm water come to life with a massive explosion is fishing at its finest. There is, however, a technique to this type of fishing. Most people, when they see the bass strike, they immediately set the hook. Big mistake. You just missed another one. The art to catching bass on a buzz bait is not to set the hook when you see the bass strike, but to wait until you feel the tug. The time between the two may only be a second, but it's the difference between success and failure. It is a hard discipline for some because we are so used to responding immediately to sight. It looks like a strike. It looks like I've got him. It looks like he's on. But he's not. Not until you feel the tug.

This is a great lesson for life. Most of the time, we live our life according to what we see. And we react accordingly. We think whatever the circumstances "look like" that is what they must be. If it looks hopeless, it must be. If it looks like the end, it must be. If it looks like there is no way out, there must not be. And we react accordingly.

There is, however, a mechanism that God has placed within us. It's a tug. It's the voice of God saying, "Don't walk by sight, but by faith." It is Him saying "Don't ever count the situation hopeless until I have been added to the equation."

71

Friend, don't set the hook on your circumstances at the first sight of trouble, but wait on the tug of God and He will turn every situation into one that is worth keeping.

ARE YOU POOR?

I thought I'd share with you what one reader shared with me. I hope you enjoy.

One day a father of a very wealthy family took his son on a trip to the country with the firm purpose of showing his son how poor people live. They spent a couple of days and nights on the farm of what would be considered a very poor family. On their return from their trip, the father asked his son, "How was the trip?"

"It was great, Dad.."

"Did you see how poor people live?" the father asked.

"Oh yeah," said the son.

"So, tell me, what did you learn from the trip?" asked the father.

The son answered: "I saw that we have one dog and they had four. We have a pool that reaches to the middle of our garden and they have a creek that has no end. We have imported lanterns in our garden and they have the stars at night. Our patio reaches to the front yard and they have the whole horizon. We have a small piece of land to live on and they have fields that go beyond our sight. We have servants who serve us, but they serve others. We buy our food, but they grow theirs.

We have walls around our property to protect us; they have friends to protect them."

The boy's father was speechless.

Then his son added, "Thanks Dad, for showing me how poor we are."

Too many times, we forget what we have and concentrate on what we don't have. What is one person's worthless object is another's prize possession. It is all based on one's perspective.

Makes you wonder what would happen if we all gave thanks for all the bounty we have instead of worrying about wanting more. Take joy and appreciate every single thing you have, especially God's great outdoors.

FREEDOM

Thomas Paine wrote concerning our freedom; "That which we obtain too cheap, we esteem too lightly; it is dearness only that gives every thing its value." That statement could be applied to many things in our lives, whether it's our freedom to own a gun and hunt, or our freedom to worship, or even our freedom of speech. It does seem that many times we "esteem these things too lightly," because many of us have "obtained" them at a price paid by someone else or one "obtained" at a very cheap cost to ourselves.

When I think about that statement, I think of all of those who are overseas, who are paying the price for the freedoms that you and I are enjoying here and now. I'm so thankful that the soil that I turn is not full of land mines and the skies that I stand in awe of are not filled with bombers and fighter jets. I'm so thankful that I am not under a dictatorship and that my money and goods are not distributed equally among everyone else. The price of these freedoms was not obtained cheap, and neither are they protected that way. As you have heard, "freedom is not free."

Outdoorsmen and outdoorswomen ought to be the most patriotic people around and our children ought to be the same. We must not only teach them to hunt and fish and enjoy the outdoors, but to respect and honor those who carry a gun into a foreign land so we can carry one into a familiar one. But not only are our military protecting freedom, they are also providing it to anyone who will take it. Why? Because freedom is not an American property and we are not its owners. We are simply one of its stewards.

Freedom is a gift of God for everyone. To keep it to ourselves would be like having the cure for cancer and yet not sharing it with the world. Freedom makes us obligated. Sometimes the cure is painful. Just ask those who have gone through chemotherapy or radiation. But the pain will lead to a better life.

May God bless all of those who enjoy freedom. May God bless all who yearn for freedom.

And may God bless all of those who are protecting and providing freedom.

A LEGACY AND A LONGING

A recent picture that I had not seen in several years brought an uncontrollable smile to my face. It was my son and me leaning against one another and him holding up a squirrel by the tail. It was his first. There he was, a seven year old with his camouflage on, his dad's hat that had been taken up to its smallest possible size, and a smile that could only be understood by people like you and me. I remember propping up that 410 on my shoulder because it was too heavy for him to hold still long enough to shoot. And I remember that squirrel hitting the ground. To me, it was if he had just hit the game winning home run or sank a last second 3 pointer. I couldn't have been more proud. A hunter's legacy had been passed on. That feeling I knew, would never leave him. It may be diluted by time or deadened by toil, but that unforgettable rush would tattoo his heart for life. Since that time, there have been many other times that he has felt compelled to go back and resurrect those emotions. That's what brings all of us back to the woods or the lakes. It is the hopes of reviving a racing heart that can only come from a bent rod or bow.

There is also a longing in the heart of man to go back to the place where we first discovered God. You may have let that relationship be diluted by time or deadened by toil. But nevertheless, it is still there. You'll never forget how your heart pounded at your first encounter with Him. And no other activity or event will ever take its place. The worst thing that you can do is ignore it. The best thing you can do is embrace it and let God revive His life in you.

FISHING IN THE DEEP

The summer presents a real challenge for the bass fisherman. For most of us "non- professional" types, it's a time that we fish on the edges; either the edge of morning or the edge of dark. It seems that the fish are more willing to feed at these times. It's different, however, for the hardcore bass fisherman. He can catch fish at two o'clock in the afternoon with a ninety degree sun beating on his back. His tactics are different. While I am casting at a place that "looks" good, he is locating, first, where the bass are. After finding them, he proceeds to try to give them what they want. While I am moving and throwing my arm off, he is patiently working the area that he knows is holding fish. While I am set on throwing that spinner bait as many times as I can, he is content to slowly drag his Carolina rig across the, seemingly, most unlikely places. I am shallow, he is deep. At the end of the day, I'm usually frustrated and he is usually overjoyed.

Sometimes, in our Christian lives, there are summer times. Times that the presence of God seems hard to find except on the edges. Times that the heat of circumstances or situations makes Him difficult to "catch." It's at that time that He calls us to move away from the bank and cast out into the deep. It's at that time that He wants us to locate where *He's* at work. It's at that time that He wants us to stay still and patient, yet persistent. Who'll be able to do this? Only those who are not satisfied to be "weekend fishermen." But those whose whole lives are spent seeking Him.

Are you having a hard time finding Him? Perhaps you're fishing in the wrong place. He may have been there before, but now He's moved out a little further. Not to leave you, but to call you out into the deep.

A GOOD WOMEN

In the middle of summer, it seems that every fisherman has become nocturnal. Most bass tournaments now begin at dark and run through the night. It seems, as I have gotten older, that I had rather sleep than fish this way. But I do find a way to do it a few times each year.

There is something about night fishing that is exciting. The lakes are calm and quiet; the skiers are non existent, and the possibility of catching a big one is always there. It also seems that your senses are sharper and that your patience runs longer. It is a different experience. If the fish are biting, sleep can wait. If the fish are not cooperating, the bottom of the boat looks as good as a king size mattress. There's nothing like slow-rolling a spinner bait across a point and getting your arm broken by a big fish. And there is equally nothing like worming a rock pile and setting the hook on an aggressive lunker. And it's all done under a blacklight. I really do love it. I just wish that my body could take more of it. Most of the time, if the fishing gets slow, we pack it in around two o'clock in the morning, and get home an hour later. If you need a lot of sleep, this is not for you; unless it's on a Friday night.

I try to convince my wife that hunting and fishing are "work." I come home tired and dirty. I have toiled in the pursuit. I even sing, "sixteen tons and what do you get, another day older and deeper in debt." I have spent untold amounts of effort and energy. And most of the time, I have received too little for the time involved. I tell her that it's rough, but "somebody's got to do it." I present my case with lawyer-type precision........She is not impressed. But it's always fun trying. I'm just thankful that she lets me go. It's good to come home to a woman like that. After twenty five years, she still puts up with me, and my nights on the lake and my days in the woods.

Solomon said, "Who can find a virtuous and capable wife? She is worth more than precious rubies. Her husband can trust her, and she will greatly enrich his life. She will not hinder him but help him all her life."

What I love about her is that she will read these wonderful words that I'm saying about her.......... and still be unimpressed.

PUBLIC SERVICE ANNOUNCEMENT

E ven though we all prepare for deer season differently, I think we can actually break down every male hunter's preparation thought pattern into 2 different categories; those who are married and those who aren't. Those who aren't married are thinking of bows, clothes, and hunting shows. Those who are married are thinking of dues, clues, and "honey do's." Like … where am I going to get enough money to buy licenses for 3 states, how am I going to let her know I need a new pair of boots, and what minor home repairs can I do in order to lessen the shock of another hunting season. You can tell that I've been married nearly 25 years. And after these many years, I have it down to a fine art.

Men, now is the time to make sure the garage is clean, the faucets are not leaking and there is a fresh coat of paint on the living room wall. It's also a good time to say, "Honey, there's a good movie on the Lifetime channel tonight; you want to watch it with me?" Start doing this periodically about 6-8 weeks prior to the first bow season. On the fourth week say, "Honey, I just saw in the paper where the mall is having a ladies shoe sale; do you want to go?" This will not only "seal the deal" but it will also plant the seed for those new boots. (ladies shoes/ hunting boots, hunting boots/ ladies shoes) Do you get the picture?

Men, remember what they say about "if mama ain't happy" and adjust accordingly.

This particular article could be put under the heading of "Public Service Announcement." I'm just looking out for your good. But remember, you must not let your wife see it! And please don't show it to mine! Read it, memorize it, chew it up, and swallow it. But some day........... Thank me.

CARP

As a youngster, the only fishing I ever did was for carp. During the summer months, it was very common to find a bunch of us boys on the banks of the canal, lined up, as if there were an annual "carp run." I can still remember the art of catching carp. After casting, we reeled in most of the excess line. If that fish was going to take the bait, he would straighten out the line. But that wasn't the time to set the hook. After the line went straight, it would sag again. When it sagged, we picked up our rod and got ready because we knew that when that line straightened again, he was on.

I can remember walking miles back home with a stringer of carp, as proud of my quarry as I could be. I thought this was as good as it gets. Later, in life, I began to catch other fish like bass, crappie, and walleye. And, to this day, I have never gone carp fishing again. You ask, "Why?" That question isn't hard to answer. It's simply because once I experienced something better than carp, I never wanted to go back. I often say that the reason my dog likes dog food, is because he has never tasted steak. It's the same principle.

It's also the way it is in many peoples' lives. They live day after day, apart from God, and think that life is good. They are as loud and proud as I was with my stringer of carp. The problem is that they will never know the difference until they have experienced the "steak" of life. A Bass fisherman is no *better* than a carp fisherman. He has only experienced something that *is* better. And he doesn't want to go back.

CLOUDS

Every area of the country has its own unique beauty. Whether it's the mountains or plains, the lakes or rivers, or the rolling hills and valleys, we all have something in nature that we claim as special. It tends to identify our part of the country. When I think of the west, I think of the massive territories filled with snow-capped peaks and long, wide prairies. When I look south, I think of everything from swamps to pines, to the beautiful Gulf. And even to the cactus filled sendaroes of Texas. When my mind wanders to the Midwest, I see the wind blowing through the acres of wheat fields. The north is equally as blessed by either mountains or flatland as far as you can see. And when I look at my own area, I see the hardwoods of Appalachia separated by the grassy valleys. It all screams the existence of a power greater than us.

One of the things however, that is common to all of us, is clouds. Some desert areas may only see a few, but they are there too. I believe God meant it that way. There's a neat scripture in the bible that says: "The LORD has His way in the whirlwind and in the storm. And the clouds are the dust of His feet."

This tells me why clouds are everywhere. It's because God is everywhere. And not only is He everywhere, He has just passed through. That's why we see this "dust". On sunny days this "dust" is scattered and may only linger around in certain areas. But on stormy days, this "dust" is concentrated and obvious.

When storms in your life come, look up to the clouds. They are the dust of the feet of God that tells you He has already been there and passed through, and made a way for you through your difficult times.

FOLLOWING IN HIS STEPS

During the end of summer, the local lake levels begin to drop, making for great fishing.

For many years I have taken this opportunity to forgo a boat and simply wade. It is the most productive fishing I have ever done. The stories and memories are numerous.

As a little boy, my son would go with me. It was a great opportunity for him to "play" in the water as well as catch fish. The water was always warm and the slope of the bank never caused a concern over him falling off of a steep ledge. There were, however, some instructions that I would always give. He was to follow in my footsteps. Even though there were no steep places, there were occasional rocks and stumps that must be maneuvered successfully in order to keep from falling. That was my job. I would look, feel, and slowly move ahead, charting a safe path for my child. To him, it may have looked like I was taking a longer or more difficult path. But I was simply leading him around the obstacles that he never knew laid ahead. His obedience and joy proved that he trusted his father. As I watched him, I was given the picture of what it really meant to trust God with a child-like faith.

Many times I have not understood the paths that I have been led down. I have even wondered why His path seemed so "out of the way." But it has been those times that I have lost the joy of the journey and the destination. My son was not concerned about obstacles. He was simply obedient. He knew and I knew that I would never lead him where I could not keep him. That is exactly the kind of relationship God wants to have with me. One that recognizes that my job is to trust Him by following in His footsteps; knowing that He will never, never, never, lead me where He cannot keep me.

BLOOM WHERE YOU'RE PLANTED

When I first began bass fishing as a young adult, I didn't have the luxury of a bass boat and all of its frills. I fished with a friend who had a "V" hull aluminum boat. The trolling motor was small and the outboard was even smaller. He owned a small cabin on the lake so our fishing always started from the same location. Because of the limited horsepower, we rarely traveled very far away. We always fished in the same places and seldom went home empty handed.

It seems as I got older and better equipped, I traveled farther and farther up and down the lake to find those illusive bass, only to have, pretty much, the same results. You see, now I spend more of my time moving than I do fishing and while I can see what's below now with a "fish finder," I once knew what was below by experience. I had fished Straight Creek Hollow so many times, under so many situations that I knew where the bass were probably hiding. I was simply forced to bloom where I was planted. Oh, there were times that I wished that I were up in the river or down beside the bridge; but I was forced to learn to succeed where I was at.

I think about this same scenario when I deer hunt. I know that I will be better off if I will just come to know the 50 acres I've been given instead of trying to hunt 400 acres.

I can remember taking a picture of a young pine tree. It was growing from the middle of a huge rock. And it was thriving. What it couldn't go around, or above, or under, it just went through. I knew that it was not suppose to grow there, but it didn't. I knew that it was out of place, but it didn't. I could have explained to it every reason why it would never become a fruitful tree, but the only thing that would have been unfruitful were my words. Because, you see, it bloomed where it was planted.

Don't let anyone tell you that you will never succeed where you're at. Take God with you. And what you can't go around, above, or under, He will take you through.

TAKE YOUR KID HUNTING

I have learned over the years from raising three children that there is a generation gap that keeps us as parents from "fitting in" with our kids. My daughters tell me not to wear certain things because they are no longer stylish. (They really don't want me to embarrass them). I try to play basketball with my son, but my older body seems to revert back to its clumsy adolescent years. The spirit is willing but the flesh is weak. It seems that no matter how hard I try to be a participator, I can only be a spectator.

As we get older, many of the things that we do with our children are things we do simply because we want to be with them and not because we actually like the activity.

But I have found one thing that bridges the gap between my son and me. It's hunting. And it's something that we both actually like to do! And not only do I see it in my life, but I see it in families all over the area. Granddads and grandsons, fathers and daughters, all have found this one thing that both can participate in and enjoy together.

Hunting is one of the few activities that does this. It causes granddads, dads and sons, all to talk and laugh and share about the same thing with equal enthusiasm.

How important is this? It is immeasurable when it comes to the need for dads to be with their children. It keeps children from the people and places that are bad influences and builds a bond that will last a lifetime.

Dad, if you want an activity that you both will enjoy and will draw you closer to each other, then "take your kid hunting instead of hunting for your kid."

DEEP ROOTS AND
GREAT FRUIT

Each year, during September and early October, I have the unique privilege of getting fed from a special drive up window. It has been a faithful server for many years. As I travel to my favorite hunting spot, I'm able to stop briefly on the gravel road, long enough to stick my hand out of the window to pick one of the hundreds of pears that this little tree produces. I usually eat one for breakfast and grab another one for a mid-morning snack. They are truly delicious. I even look forward to seeing them from year to year. I can't tell you what species they are, only that they are sweet and good.

Recently, I've thought about how blessed I am to be able to feed at such a humble place. I've thought about how most people will never experience such an event and how much like Heaven this must be.

I can imagine driving down the streets of gold in my four-wheel drive pickup and reaching out to take not only a pear, but an apple and an orange, and a banana. And yes, there will be trucks in Heaven. But I think what amazes me most about this pear tree, is its appearance. To look at this tree in the winter or early spring, you wouldn't be very proud of its stature or very confident about its ability to produce. It's scraggly and short. Its limbs have been broken down from years of holding up those heavy pears. The leaves remind me of those of us who are losing our hair. They are patchy and thin. No, there's not much about this tree that would tell me that anything worthwhile, would ever come from such an unlikely candidate. No awards from the Arbor Foundation for this puppy. And yet, what comes from its bony hands, are gems.

Perhaps, when others look at you, they also see an unlikely candidate for anything worthwhile. You may even look in the mirror and agree with them. "Surely, nothing great could come from me." But you see, what makes that little pear tree produce year after year has nothing to do with its outside appearance, but it has everything to do with what it has put its roots in; underneath, where we cannot see.

Jesus said, "He who abides in Me, bears much fruit."

CONSIDER THE RAVENS

You may think that sitting in the deer woods, in a tree stand, is boring. It's anything but boring. When the sun comes up, the community of animals and insects goes to work. The night shift is going home and the day shift is making his way to the job at hand. It's another day on the wilderness expressway. Every creature has a particular purpose.

It may be the "stay at home" doe whose daily task is raising and protecting that young fawn that can't seem to keep its nose out of everything. It may be the chipmunk who sprints from one place to another, gathering up the materials to "winterize" its home. Or it may be the small spider who will patiently spin its web at the nearest "food mart" in order to provide the necessary sustenance.

Sounds like us, doesn't it? But, if you look closer, you will see a major difference. In the animal world, there are no signs of worry or stress, or doubt. They are persistent, yes. But they make time everyday for fun, fellowship and even naps. They know that it is the God of the universe who will provide for them. He always has, so there is no need to worry, doubt or get "stressed out."

It seems that they know that the Bible says, "Consider the ravens, for they neither sow nor reap, which have neither storehouse nor barn; and God feeds them." And it seems they have read where the scripture says, "Consider the lilies, how they grow: they neither toil nor spin."

I wonder if WE know the rest of that verse: "If then God so clothes the grass, which today is in the field and tomorrow is thrown into the oven, how much more will He take care of you." You know, I have never seen an animal worry. Have you?

LISTENING THROUGH THE NOISE

If the non-hunter sits in the woods, he hears nothing. To sit a hunter in the woods, he hears everything. The woods are not silent. They are full with the sounds of the language of a world man is not a part of.

I have jumped out of my hunting boots at times at the sound of a hoot owl before dawn, while the rest of the animal residents go on about their business at the same sound.

In the tree stand, one must learn to hear "through" certain sounds. The woods are loud with the gobble of a turkey, the cutting of a squirrel, the caw of a crow, and a host of other sounds from birds, insects and other critters. But the hunter must learn to hear "through" those sounds in order to hear the quiet movement of a deer. It is crucial to be still and quiet and to listen.

We also live in a world that is full of sounds. They are a part of our daily lives. They come from our jobs, our homes, and our friends. Some sounds are nothing more than the noise from a T.V. or a radio. And yet in all of this, God is also speaking to us. It's a voice that is plain and yet cannot be heard, unless you are listening for it. Can you hear Him? If not, maybe it's because you have not stopped long enough to be quiet, and listen "through" the sounds of the world, to hear the "still small voice" of God, calling for an encounter with you.

BEING READY FOR THE DAY

In Tennessee, deer season is just around the corner. There's a frantic pace in most hunters' homes right now. It's caused by the pressure of preparation. Even though we may have been shooting our bows for a while now, those last minute things have been left for well…… the last minute. Do I have enough clothes and are they all washed in some scent eliminator? Do my boots have one more year of service in them? Do I have broadheads and bullets? And where have I put my climbing harness? It's all part of each year's ritual. I wonder sometimes why I don't just get better organized at the *end* of the season so I will already be prepared for the next? But that would be too easy.

I do know this, however; I have a lot more peace and contentment and satisfaction when I know that I am ready. And we hunters must always be ready to go. We never know when a two hour opportunity may arise that will allow us to spend an afternoon in the place we love. And when that is the case, every minute counts. There can be no fumbling around in mind or body. We must be prepared to grab our bow and a bottle of water and "hit" the woods.

Over the years, I have also seen those who live their lives spiritually unprepared. They know that the day is coming (and may be around the corner) when God's day of harvest will come. It may come when we die or when He chooses to come back. But it's coming. And most people are unprepared. They are living with the belief that one day they will make last minute preparation. I hope they will. But the problem with that belief is that we don't know when this "season" will officially open. It's only known and determined by God. But how much more peace and contentment and satisfaction there is knowing that whenever He chooses to "open", we will have already taken spiritual inventory and made sure we were ready.

MY NASCAR MOMENT

I rose early that morning, slightly before my Big Ben went off. I slipped quietly into my Hush Puppies and headed to my Mansfield commode. The Phillips 60 watt, 130 volt light bulb worked perfectly. After fixing my Martha White, self-rising, blueberry muffins, I headed back down stairs. There in my Rubbermaid container were the clothes I would choose for my morning hunt. First, the Fruit of the Loom "essentials," and then layer by layer of Mothwing Fall Mimicry camo mixed with just the right amount of the spring pattern as well. I shed my Hush Puppies and donned my Lacrosse, 500 gram Burley boots. I grabbed a snack and a drink and stuffed them into my Cabelas backpack. I drove frantically in my Nissan Pathfinder but I new I was safe thanks to my 15 inch Hankook, Dynapro tires.

After stopping at Hardees' for my Maxwell House cup of coffee, I finally arrived at the farm I would hunt that morning. After listening to the weather report on my Panasonic am, fm, cd/cassette/ 8 track player radio, I knew it would be a great day.

It didn't take long to find the tree I would climb. I wrapped my API Grand Slam Magnum treestand around its base and slowly ascended while moving my Hunter Specialty safety harness up as I went.

Once there, I checked my Newberry B1 bow, careful to give extra attention to my Trophy Taker drop away rest and fiber optics sight.

It wasn't long before I heard the rustle of leaves. I raised my Alpen Apex 8 x 42 binoculars and, sure enough, a deer was approaching. I aimed my Bushnell 500 Range Finder and marked a 25 yard shot. When the deer passed by, I launched my 400 gram Easton Carbon arrow. The deer fell. I spent the next 30 minutes in that tree stand eating my Little Debbie cake and drinking my Cumberland Gap water thinking how wonderful it is to have the opportunity to be able to enjoy hunting just as my forefathers did.

I would like to thank all of my sponsors who gladly sell their stuff to Wal-Mart and other fine department stores, so I can buy them there. And I would also like to say hi to my mom and give thanks to God for giving me the ability to do what I do.

TROPHIES OF HIS GRACE

It seems now a day that many of us are into hunting the "trophy," especially those of you who have been hunting for a long time. To take a doe or a small buck no longer interests you. I'm not there yet. And I suppose there are more hunters out there, just like me. I still get a thrill out of taking a doe with a bow.

Now I have never claimed to be a hunting expert, nor one who can claim many hunting experiences and adventures. I just love to hunt. The "trophy" for me is simply success.

It doesn't take long to see that trophies come in different sizes to different people. Just look at the pictures that adorn the check-in stations and you will see the smiling faces of youth and adults alike. Some are not even old enough to hold up a gun by themselves. There are girls in pigtails, boys in their dads' clothes and older folks, all with the same proud look. Some are kneeling beside a doe, others a spike, and some a real "rocking chair rack." But the one thing in common is they all have their trophy.

Sometimes it may seem that God has *His* trophies, those who are spiritually bigger than you and me. Men and women who, it seems, are more loved by God. They seem to have position and possessions and no problems. What they bring to God's check-in station is so much bigger than what we bring. But we are so wrong.

God has never culled or passed on one member of His creation. We are all loved, gifted and special to Him. As you have heard many times, if we were the only person on earth,

God would have sent His son to die for us. That makes us all a trophy of His grace.

PRICELESS DIVIDENDS

A few weeks ago, I peeked in on a hunter safety course that was being taught by our local game warden. It was a joy to see participants of all ages. I saw those who were ten years old and those who, I know were pushing seventy. Some were grandparents who were bringing grand-children and some were parents bringing their children. It's always good to see the hunting legacy being passed on. The course is not made to be difficult. It's meant to simply teach the basics of gun safety in the woods. It's a shame that more adults don't take their youngsters to such an event. It's the only way we will preserve the hunting lifestyle.

Even though my daughters don't hunt, they have both earned their diploma and have insured their right to hunt if they ever chose to do so. My son has also finished the course and hunts regularly with me. There is no cost but the dividends are priceless. Your child may never hunt, but without graduating from this class, he or she will never get the opportunity. And if a generation of children fails to hunt, their children will, most likely, do the same. I hope and pray this never happens. But, it will if we as parents and grand-parents don't insist on their participation.

Many of you can remember days past, when you were exposed to hunting. Now, years have past, you've gotten busy, and hunting is something that you no longer do. Your memories of that time, however, are good. Why not give your child that same opportunity? Why not let them experi-ence what you did? You were not scarred or traumatized and neither will they be. In fact, they may find something that is so invigorating that it causes them to find their "high" some-where besides in a drug or drink.

There are two things that I have exposed my children to, that I am most proud of; a faith in Christ and an opportunity to take a gun or bow into the woods. Both will give them a lifetime full of adventurous excitement.

THE BLOOD TRAIL

Some of you have already filled a tag. I have seen the trophy in your truck or strapped across your car. You may be like me, and "happen to have" a picture with you to show to an unsuspecting (and sometimes uninterested) friend. For us, it's not just the prize, but it's the process! The story. The experience.

One thing we have all learned is...... the work begins **after** the shot.

I called my first deer, this year, the Star Trek doe. It literally went where no man had gone before. I had to go through Ekos and fight two Klingons, to get that deer back to my truck. Was it hard? Yes! Was it exhausting? Definitely! Was it necessary? Most definitely! But was it worth it? Absolutely!

You see, to be a hunter means that you must finish the job. To find that deer at the end of the trail of blood is an unexplainable experience. But the deer must be taken out. It is our responsibility.

I remember a time in my life when a trail of blood led to a cross. It was at that cross that I found the greatest prize. What I realized there was that the cross and its story were not meant to stay there. I was not there to simply admire it or keep it to myself. But it was now my responsibility to get it out.

Hunter friend, the next time you drag a deer from the woods, ask yourself if you are making the same effort in getting out the greatest story ever told. Yes, it will be hard. Yes, it will be exhausting. But it is necessary and it is absolutely worth it to those who have never heard the good news of the gospel.

CAMOUFLAGE

Camouflage is the great equalizer for hunters. It comes in several different brands, patterns and styles. Its job is to create an illusion in the eyes of the deer so that it doesn't know you are there. It also works on other animals. I have had to duck and dodge to keep birds and squirrels at bay.

Camouflage patterns cause most animals to have a problem with depth perception. They see something, but they can't seem to focus in good enough to know that something is wrong. Simply put, camouflage plants us in their world.

Even though we are in their world, we are not of their world. We can dress the part, hide, and even utter some of the same sounds, but we are only taking up temporary space in a place that is not our home. It's not that we don't enjoy their world; we do. In fact, we wish that we could spend more time in it. But it's the fact that no matter how hard we try, we can never fully be a part of a place that we were not built for.

That's also the way Christians are to live their lives. The Bible says that we are in the world, but not of the world. That is, we may look, dress, talk and fit in this world on many occasions, but we must always remember that we were not built for earth, but for heaven. You and I will never feel completely comfortable "down here." It's not that we don't enjoy this place or that we want to leave it prematurely, but it's just the fact that we were built for heaven. And not only "Christians," but every one of us was made for a world that is better than the one that we are in. It's just that some have already made plans to arrive.

MY ADMMISSION

Climbing into a tree stand can be an uneasy experience. It seems that no matter how many years I've been doing it, I still get a little bit squeamish every time I ascend to that 20 x 30 inch platform. It doesn't help when I think that every part of that stand was probably provided by the lowest bidder. And the safety harnesses of times past were more of a fancy noose than a real "restraint system." They would have simply left you hanging, upside down, waiting on someone to come and field dress you. They were probably made by the deer, just for revenge.

For some odd reason, I always think of a certain scripture when I'm up in a tree. Jesus said, "lo I am with you always'. He didn't say anything about *high*!

It's because of this fear that I have become a full-fledged "tree hugger." Yes, I'm finally admitting it. After years of feeling the urge, I am coming out of the closet. WHEN I'M UP IN A TREE, I HUG IT FOR DEAR LIFE! Wow, I feel better just talking about it!

But why the tree? Why not my backpack or my bow or even my tree stand? Well, it's because that tree is attached to the ground; the place I know and trust. It has its roots deep within the soil. It has a sure foundation. And while it may bend or bow, it will not break. That is what I want to be attached to.

Our lives are to be the same way. They are to be attached to something that is sure and steadfast, unmovable and unshakable. And while the winds may blow, because our roots are planted deep, we may bend and bow, but we will not break.

What is that foundation that is sure and does not change? It is nothing less than Christ. He is the foundation that all of our lives are to be built upon because He is the same; yesterday, today and forever. And while our world and all that's in it may change.....He will not. And you can hang your stand on that!

CAMARADERIE

If you have hunted long enough, you have realized that there is camaraderie among hunters. And that camaraderie spans all sorts of social and economic boundaries. I can see a stranger in camouflage and talk to him as if we are long lost friends. The terminology we all use is universal.

Hunting brings together the rich and the poor, the executive and the laborer, the popular and the common. I like it that way. There are no big people and little people. There are only people who like to hunt. If you look at their lives at other times, they all may be different. Some will put on a tie on Monday morning. Some will slip into a doctor's gown. Some will lace up steel toe boots. And others will don a uniform.

I have hunted in several states, and hunting is *one* of the things that have made every place feel like home. The other thing is my Christianity. There is also camaraderie among Christians. Not elitism, but a relationship and a language that bring all sorts of people together on common ground. It too bridges the gap between the rich and the poor, the popular and the common, and even the northerner and the southerner. That's why we call each other "brother" or "sister." It's because we are family.

I like introducing someone to hunting. It's something anyone can be a part of. My hope for them is that they might enjoy it as much as I do.

A greater thrill is introducing someone to Christ. He invites all to come. No matter what our past has been, no matter what we may have or not have, no matter who we are or where we're from, we can have something in common that makes us all brothers and sisters, and makes every place feel like home.

THE OHIO CANOE TRIP

For the past few years I have been taking a late October deer hunting trip to Ohio. They truly have some real bruisers up there. And if you fill your tag during the rut, you'll have to do it with a conventional bow or crossbow. Not only is this a great deer hunt, it's also the most invigorating and taxing hunting trip that I take. Instead of a short drive in a pickup or four-wheeler to a hunting house, I canoe about a half mile upstream, then walk another hundred and fifty yards, and then climb up a tree where I have strategically placed a lock-on stand the day before. The weather is usually cold but the friendships and experiences that I have forged there over the years are warm.

Now, about that canoe.........

I can remember, as a young teenager, being exposed to my first canoe. I was blessed to have been taught by knowledgeable people concerning what to do and what not to do. After all, that simple boat can be very capricious. No quick movements. Distribute the weight. And remember, even though fiberglass and the newer materials may be faster, aluminum is more stable and sure.

And at forty five years old, I am no longer built for speed. I recommend aluminum.

One year, a hunting friend and I took the trip during an unusually wet season. The lazy stream that usually flowed slow and easy, was now, in my book, at least a class three rapid. Now in most instances, we would have turned and went home but we were deer hunting so we forwent the thought of any loss of life or limb and pushed our canoes into the water. Being the gentleman that I am...... I let him go first. It was the funniest sight that I think I'd ever seen. My friend, flailing, and swarping and thrashing, trying to go upstream, while the river was taking him downstream like he was not even there. He was fighting for dear life, while those of us on the bank where trying to look concerned on the outside but laughing on the inside; until we knew he was safely back on the bank, to which we then laughed out loud.

It's truly amazing to think what we're all willing to put ourselves through in order to do the things that we love the most. And I'm sure that it's equally as amazing to hear some of the excuses that we all use for not doing the things that we ought to as well.

THE PARALYSIS OF ANALYSIS

There's no doubt that the longer we have hunted, the more stories we have about the ones that got away; or worse, the ones we've missed. I think that I am pretty sure in saying that I miss at least one deer every year. The excuses abound but the results are the same.

When I think about it, it seems that the memories of my misses are more vivid than the memories of the deer that became stew.

If you're like me, you often relive your most recent miss and wish that you had it to do over. It doesn't help when you're forced to climb into that same tree stand where you just messed up the day, week, or even year before. Now, you are in that same environment again. There's that branch that deflected the arrow….. If I would have just waited until he moved to that opening……….. If I had just been a little more patient. And the list goes on.

There is one thing for sure, however; if I linger on the past too long, I will never enjoy the present. And if I allow the failures of the past to fill my mind, I will never enjoy future successes. I call this "the paralysis of analysis." It's where we think about something for so long that we never move on. It's where we let the failures of the past keep us from enjoying something in the future.

Some of you are living, right now, in this frame of mind. You have had failures in the past. It may have been with a spouse or a business deal, or with your own finances. It may be your seemingly inability to live a certain way and, as a result, you cannot make another step of faith.

Friend, don't let the misses of the past keep you from the next hunt. Don't let the failures of the past keep you from enjoying what God has for you in the future.

Failures are only meant to describe a moment in time. They are never meant to describe a person. And they don't describe you.

THE GOOD, BAD WEATHER

Have you noticed that while everyone else is enjoying the beautiful fall days, the hunter is crying "bah humbug?"

It seems everyday, lately, someone is sharing his thankfulness for the sunny and unusually warm days. Outwardly I am rejoicing with him, but inwardly I am shouting "bring on the cold and dreary days of winter." Hunters know that the best days for deer to stir seem to be when the weather is bad.

I have hunted in snow, rain, and sleet and have done it with more anticipation and success than during the days of sunshine and warmth. Yes, it takes more planning, more equipment, and more effort, but knowing that the deer will be there, makes it all worthwhile.

And then there's the thought of knowing that while all of the "fair weather" hunters are at home in their recliners, I am out in the "frozen tundra" proving that a country boy can survive.

Let me tell you that life is the same way. Even though God may move in our lives during the good times, the real movement happens when our days are dreary and cold. It seems that most of us give God very little attention when things are going well. But when there is a cloud over our day, we look to Him. So, God must bring storms into our lives. He doesn't do it because He likes to see us struggle. He does it because that's when we can best see Him move.

Are you in a storm right now? Has your sunny fall weather turned into an overcast and cold day? Let me tell you what to do. Go hunting, not for deer, but for God. You will find that He will be stirring.

ONE OF MY BEST DAYS

As I was glassing the field, I glanced to my left and noticed the buck coming down the hill. He was close so I didn't have much time to get ready. I could already feel the warmth come over me from my accelerated heart beat. I put my binoculars down and grabbed my rifle. By that time I was almost hyperventilating. I could only manage short, choppy breaths. Trying to talk was even worse. It wasn't like I had not been in this situation before, but I so wanted success that my nervousness was magnified.

The buck was not a "wall hanger." I had even passed on taking it just a few days before. But now the timing was right and the opportunity might not come again. I picked my binoculars back up and watched as the buck headed directly toward me.

If the deer would just turn broadside, a shot could be made. After a few steps he decided to oblige. I could see, however, that he was getting ready to turn his walk into a trot. I had to act quickly. With grunt tube in hand, I softly called. He stopped and stared long enough for the perfect shot to be placed. I watched as he ran down the hill knowing that he wouldn't go far.

All of the nervousness and hyperventilating immediately turned into an overwhelming joy. I almost couldn't contain it. It was coming out of my body. It showed up in my hands, legs, feet and face. I had not felt exactly that way in some time. It was so noticeable that I made a conscience effort to enjoy the enjoyment. With the recent week of stress and problems, I wanted to stay in that moment as long as I could. And I did.

I had just had a front row seat as my son had taken another deer. I had watched him do, with precision, exactly what he had been taught to do. I had been there to see the same joy come over him that had come over me. And I know that it has made a wonderfully indelible mark that will continually call him back to the hunt.

A MATTER OF PREPARATION

When it begins to get cold, preparation is of paramount importance. There is nothing worse than having to leave a hunting stand because the cold weather has won out. And there is no better feeling than being out in the freezing weather and enjoying it. Again, it's a matter of preparation.

I learned how to stay warm the hard way. I can remember when I began hunting deer years ago; I would get out of my truck and put on every stitch of clothes I could find, before I walked into the woods. I looked like an orange Michelin man. The sightings of Bigfoot that you thought you saw..... were me. By the time that I walked several hundred yards (or sometimes miles) to my stand, I would be sweating so much that deer smelled me in three counties. And then I would sit. And sit. And sit. Do you know what water turns to in sub zero temperatures? That's right, ice! So there I was now, an orange frozen Popsicle. What time was it? 8:00 a.m. Oh, those were the days! Needless to say, I never did much good.

I'm glad that I learned what to wear, when to wear it, and what to bring with me.

But why do I want, so much, to be prepared? So I can last through any type of weather; good or bad.

In my Christian life, I also want to last. I don't want to give up when the "weather" turns bad or when things are cold and tough. I want to last! I want to last so I don't miss one blessing that may cross my path. I want to last so that I don't miss one experience that may go with me through a lifetime. I'm glad that God has given us everything we need to last. And it's found in His word.

THE EXPERTS

It still amazes me when I think of what I'm actually willing to go through to hunt. Within the last week, I have spent time in the tree stand with a stomach virus and, as I write, I'm in that same stand with a sprained ankle. And now it's raining! Both the ankle and the virus left me so weak that I could barely make it up onto my lofty perch. I laugh while really considering what it is that causes me to do this. My wife just shakes her head.

Where I live, we are in the first few days of the peak rut. That incentive alone is a miraculous healer. Have you ever noticed how we can fish all night but fall to sleep on the couch at 9:00 p.m. when we're at home? Have you ever noticed that we'll get up before the alarm goes off when we're going hunting, but at other times we keep hitting the snooze bar? I think if the "higher ups" really studied it, we might find that we hunter-fisher types have a new disease! Maybe then we could get the government to pay us for our "suffering."

I think the reason that I continually go even under adverse circumstances is because I've been trying to do as the experts tell me. They say it's best to hunt just before a rain, just after a rain, and in the rain. I'm supposed to go before a cold front and after one. They tell me the best time to kill a big buck will be during the pre-rut, post-rut and during the rut. If the moon is full, hunt through lunch. If the moon is new, hunt all day. Early in the season, hunt in the evening. And late in the season, hunt in the morning. Heck! I think that just about covers em' all!

I figure, that between August and January and from Alabama to Michigan, I ought to hunt everyday. And as sure as I miss a day, that will be the day that the big one passes through.

I think I'll gather my stuff and limp back to the truck. It stopped raining. It stopped raining?

I'd better stay.

IT'S SNOWING SOMEWHERE

I love hunting in the snow. Deer can be seen from hundreds of yards away and the snow seems to muffle all of the usual sounds that come from a distance. It is a different hunt. The deer are no longer foraging in the fields but are looking for the browse that grows in the fence lines and above the new fallen snow. Sometimes they travel later in the day in order to let the sun "warm up" breakfast. It can get very cold out there, but that's the price you pay for hunting. (It's a hard job, but someone has to do it.)

Snow has two affects. It exposes and conceals. It doesn't take long to see a brown deer move across white snow. Its color and movement are magnified against the pale background. But what about "under" the snow? Have you noticed how snow hides every flaw of earth? Like a blanket, the snow covers every crook, crevice, and cranny of the ground. It conceals everything that it falls upon.

There is an overwhelming comparison between God's grace and the purity of snow. Our sins, laid against the backdrop of God's grace, are exposed and magnified like the deer against the snow. But when those sins are "under" His grace, they are concealed and covered. They are blanketed and hid just as the snow hides the scars of earth.

Hunter friend, let me ask you……. Are your sins exposed by His grace, or have they been covered by His grace? God's grace, like snow, will hide every scar if you will let it fall on you.

Remember that as long as there is a scar to be covered, somewhere in God's kingdom…... it's snowing.

HAVING IT BOTH WAYS

I've always been a country boy at heart. And even though I longed to leave in my high school years, there was something that drew me back to the humble surroundings of my country way of living.

It's not always easy balancing this lifestyle with progress. It almost doesn't seem right to want a rustic log cabin with a microwave. I want cows and dogs but a big screen T.V. would be nice as well. And I'm sure that even though my wife wants a clothes line in the back yard, she sure couldn't do without her heavy duty washer and dryer. I want a garden, but I'd sure rather plow it with a new John Deere rather than an old mule.

One of the things that is especially troubling to me is the loss of much of our hunting land. Where there used to be deer and ducks, now there are malls and mansions. Where there used to be the sycamore and sassafras, now there are subdivisions. It's all in the name of progress. I think everyone ought to experience the joy and peace of country living. I just don't want them to enjoy it so much that they buy my hunting lease, build their retirement home, and turn MY property into an animal sanctuary. But the fact is I can't have it both ways. I can't fuss about my dirt road without knowing that pavement is going to bring people. And I can't fuss about not having city conveniences without having the city.

Many churches today, struggle with this same dilemma. They want people without progress. They want big buildings without big budgets. And they want "sinners" without sin. They've forgotten the invitation to come "Just as I am," but instead have asked folks to come "just as they would like to be, one day." They've forgotten that we are not to come to the Lord clean, but we are to come to Him and let Him clean us up. They've forgotten that Jesus was a friend of sinners.

So if you and I want others to experience our life in the Lord, remember that you're going to have to move over. You're going to have to bring them in as they are. And you might just have to give them your parking space and your pew.

"THE BARN"

On cold and windy days, I love to hunt from "the barn." I have two square bales stacked on top of one another on which to rest my gun. And I sit on a third bale. Because this set-up is in the loft of the barn, I have a great view of the fields below. There have been a few mornings that I have climbed up top only to be greeted by other occupants of the critter variety. I have never actually seen one, but I have heard them quickly scamper toward the nearest exit. Most of the time, I am able to carry with me a cup of coffee and the morning newspaper which I read by flashlight. I read until there's just enough sunlight to allow me to see with my binoculars across the fields. As you can tell, it makes for a comfortable hunt. And it's not just an "easy" place to go, but I have actually taken several deer from this gigantic "tree" stand.

It's, undoubtedly, a luxury to hunt from such a place, but I can't imagine a mother giving birth to a newborn baby in that same environment. And yet that is what I'm reminded of right now. I think of Mary and Joseph being relegated to "the barn." I can imagine that Joseph may have felt guilty that he was not able to provide something better for his wife and soon-to-be mother. He must have gathered and stacked the hay in order to make the surroundings as comfortable as possible. He must have made sure that the "room" was out of the wind and that it was as clean as could be expected. But, no matter how much he tried, it was still a barn.

Would God let His child be born in a barn? Not only "would He," but He did. I wonder if that barn was still standing, what it would be worth. There's no doubt that some religious organization would give millions, not because of the worth of the barn itself, but because of the value of what happened inside.

You see, what makes our life of value is not *what's* on the outside, but it's *Who's* on the inside. And when God's Son lives within us, we become of great value to God, ourselves, and the world.

NON-TYPICAL

Have you ever noticed that many of the best bucks ever taken have been of the non-typical type? The racks of these monsters are as unique as the stories of how they made it to the "wall of fame." They come in 16, 20, and even 30 point varieties. They may have drop-tines, multiple brow tines, stickers and a host of other deformities; and yet, they are trophies that all hunters long for.

It's said that the reason these racks become non-typical is either from injury or illness, and sometimes even genetics. That is, sometime early in their development, a tragedy took place. It was one so great that it affected the entire life span of that deer. It was, undoubtedly, traumatic and perhaps even life threatening. And the scars that were left could not be hidden from friend or foe. Even though they overcame the experience, everyone would always know something bad had happened. But look what took place after that experience; the maimed became the monarch and the tragedy produced a trophy! And what was once the ugly duckling became the swan of the woods.

Herein, is a wonderful lesson. Many of you think that your tragedy is too big to overcome. The injury was too severe. The illness was too devastating. Your past is tainted with one bad decision after another. You feel that the scars of the battles have marked you as unwanted or unneeded. It seems now, that you are looked at in a different way- that you are non-typical.

Friend, God's specialty is turning the non-typical into the trophy. He mixes love, truth and time together to produce a work of His grace. Your past is His canvas and your hurts are the colors He uses to paint the picture of what He wants you to become. Don't spend your time regretting an unchangeable past. Instead, let God take it and make it into a place where He can show you off, as a trophy of grace.

THE FISHING MINISTRY

The bass fishermen are getting antsy. I can feel it. It's mid-winter and the days that are fit to fish are few and far between, and better weather is still at least a month away. The television shows aren't helping. They have shelved the deer hunting episodes and are now flooding us with one fishing show after another. The sponsors want it that way. They want to show us the latest and greatest lures now, so that when fishing is full tilt, we'll have a tackle box full of their products.

Fishing is becoming one of the fastest growing sports in our country, especially bass fishing. The "tournament trail" has touched a nerve in every red-blooded man. I don't know who came up with the idea but they knew what they were doing. You see, the "tournament" type fishing speaks to everything that a man enjoys: sports, competition, fans, winning, beating the other guy, money and prizes, and the outdoors. It's definitely a recipe for a growing sport's success. And now, there's big money in it. Who would've ever "thunk" it?

Now, more than any other time, more people are making careers out of fishing! Ain't God good! I can see it now. One day there will be college and high school fishing teams. Men and woman alike will be offered scholarship money if they will "sign" to fish for a particular school. They'll graduate with a Master's of Fishing degree and some will even go on to the pros. Only in America! What's wrong with this? Absolutely nothing. If we can have someone making a living creating video games, why can't we have someone making a living fishing? We can.

You see, it's not about what we do, but it's about Who we do it for. As long as what we do doesn't cause us to sin or someone else, then God wants you to use your talent for Him. Whether your talent is creating video games or fishing, you can use what you have, what you are, and even what you want to become as an avenue to point others to Him. Jesus called fishermen to follow Him.

CONTENTMENT

There is no doubt that the outdoors serve as a great therapy. If you have never walked out on the porch of a lake cabin and smelled the early morning breeze, you might not appreciate its worth. It clears the mind and soul and brings us back to the simpler and slower things of life.

You can't fish or hunt and be impatient. Both go against everything that we do during the rest of the week. The lives of the masses are engulfed everyday in high speed chases. We are in hot pursuit of things that we think we must have.

And then we must work more and longer days in order to maintain them.

I am discovering that the wisest people in the world are not always the most educated or the ones that "look" the part, but they are the ones who have learned that fishing is just as important as making money. They drive an hour in their 1990 paid off pickup truck to the lake. Their boat, if they own one, is designed for comfort. They may fish for bass or bluegill or crappie but they understand that success is not measured by the catch but by the opportunity to go. They have learned what most of us have forgotten …….. Contentment.

Many people say, "I couldn't sit for hours waiting on a bite from a fish or waiting to see a deer." Learn how, and then you will understand how to enjoy life and you will make better decisions in all other areas. Remember that constant going is not a sign of importance and "busyness" is not a sign of accomplishment. It only means that you have not learned what the old fisherman has…….. that godliness with contentment is great gain.

THE BALANCING ACT

I just returned from one final deer hunting trip. I know that, each year, when my Alabama adventure is over, it's time to take down tree stands and put up all of the "goodies" that have gone with me for four months. That doesn't mean that I quit hunting, but only that I change gears to accommodate the fish and wildlife commissions of each state. I'm presently trying my hand at predator hunting while waiting on the annual stripe and walleye run. Some of you are duck or grouse hunting which are also good ways to empty a loaded shotgun. The main thing is that each one of us continues to enjoy the outdoors.

My wife says the main thing is that I get on that honey-do list that has been put on the back burner while I've been pursuing deer. And since she is the president of *my* fish and game commission, I think I'll obey her laws. She's pretty lenient, most of the time, but after four months, now is not one of those times. Her laws are not made to hinder my enjoyment, only to make sure that I'm not hurting my relationship with her, the family and others. She loves me and celebrates with me during the thrilling moments of my life, but she also is a great balance to let me know when I am leaning too far to one side. It's at that time, that she tells me and she draws me back to where we both want to be.

God's laws are that way also. They are not given to us in order to hinder our enjoyment of life, but only to keep us from hindering and hurting our relationship with Him, our family and others. His laws are our protection because He has already seen the consequences of those who ignore

His words. If His words continually go unheeded, heartache and hurt comes, and enjoyment leaves. Friend, don't look at God's commands as words to hinder your enjoyment but as words of protection from someone who loves you so much that He will tell you when you are hurting the relationships that you need the most.

MORE GADGETS

W ell, it seems that deer season is coming to a halt.
Except for those down south, the rut is over and the
activity is slow. This week is the last week of hunting where
I live, so I have pulled out all of the stops. It seems, anymore,
that I have to carry a separate backpack for just the calls and
the accessories that I use today. It used to be if you had a grunt
call, rattling horns and a tree stand, you could be successful.
Now you would be considered unprepared. Today's hunter
must be equipped with everything from a barometer gauge
to a rear view mirror. I have never seen so many "must have"
gadgets in my life.

It's a must today to have a hundred dollar flashlight,
range finder and, just in cause you can't find your deer, a
game finder. The calls around my neck make me feel like a
duck hunter. When times get tough, they tell me I can lure
in a deer with one of these special calls. So now after about
thirty minutes, I start a succession of noises that sounds like
a rap artist. I grunt, bleat, rattle, snort and wheeze. I sound
like a deer with the flu! I think if I ever heard a deer do all of
these things, I wouldn't want to shoot it!

And then, there's the tree stand set-up. I'm sitting there,
under my screw-in umbrella, staring in my rear view mirror
with my feet snuggled up in blankets. My "gadget strap" is
tied around the tree and loaded down with, well...... gadgets.
I have, burning below the tree, deer incense. I have just
released a "doe in heat" smoke bomb that has been strategically placed around my mock scrape. And now I am alter-
nating between the range finder and the binoculars to see if,

perhaps, there's a deer that has temporarily lost all sense of sight and sound. I have done everything they told me to do. I just wish that I hadn't forgotten my gun.

JUST FOR DREAMERS

First light has always been my favorite time of day. It's at that time, that my expectation is at its highest. Whether I'm fishing, hunting or just out and about, I love the possibilities and excitement the breaking day brings. It seems that all game is more active during this period. Every cast is made with a great expectation. Every corner of the woods is looked at with a great expectation. The skies are filled with a great expectation. It's a feeling that only you and I know. I wonder sometimes, if that's not what draws us back to the water or the woods.

It seems that much of our daily lives are filled with, less than great, expectations. Instead, they are filled with expectations of the normal or average type. We expect to go to work, put in a long day, get off, come home, and do it all again the next day. And we usually get what we expect. But when we are in the woods or on the water our mind begins to think outside the normal possibilities. I never go into a hunt with a great expectation to shoot a spike. Nor do I rush to get to the lake so I can land that 12 inch largemouth. No, my mind soars beyond the average and beyond the normal, to the possibilities of what may lie just beyond the corner or just under the surface. And it's that *dream* that makes the experience so exciting. Some people say, "Get real." I prefer to let my mind take me to the "what ifs."

God has put within each one of us the capacity to dream. Those dreams are our motivation. They are our "great expectations." They get us up early and keep us out late. When put into action, they are our contribution to the world. They have taken us where we had never been and allowed us to do things that we thought we would never do; all because someone dreamed. If you have a dream, it's a gift from God, given to you, to be used for Him. To NOT follow *that* dream would be not only a shame, but a sin.

Printed in the United States
61899LVS00001B/1-195

9 781600 344473